ANIMAL JOURNEYS

360 DEGREES, an imprint of Tiger Tales
5 River Road, Suite 128, Wilton, CT 06897
Published in the United States 2017
Originally published in Great Britain 2017
by Caterpillar Books
Text by Patricia Hegarty
Text copyright © 2017 Caterpillar Books
Illustrations copyright © 2017 Jessica Courtney-Tickle
ISBN-13: 978-1-944530-04-4
ISBN-10: 1-944530-04-5
Printed in China
CPB/1800/0581/0916
10 9 8 7 6 5 4 3 2 1

For more insight and activities, visit us at www.tigertalesbooks.com

ANIMAL JOURNEYS

by Patricia Hegarty • Illustrated by Jessica Courtney-Tickle

INTRODUCTION

Many animals make astonishing journeys, some stretching thousands of miles, others covering only a matter of inches, but all are remarkable in their own unique way.

This book explores how some of these amazing feats are achieved, often against incredible odds and in harsh and unfriendly environments.

CONTENTS

MIRACULOUS MIGRATIONS

Some types of animals and birds set off on yearly journeys.
They travel in search of food, breeding grounds, or warmth
and often cover long distances. This is called migration.

How some of these epic journeys are achieved is still
a mystery to scientists. However, it is believed that many use
the Sun and the stars to navigate, as well as Earth's magnetic field
and natural formations such as rivers, lakes, and mountain ranges.

SUPER-COMMUTER

The Arctic tern makes the longest migration of any creature.

It flies from its breeding grounds in the Arctic to the Antarctic and back again every year.

Scientists have recorded journeys of up to 57,000 miles (91,600 km).

MAASAI MIGRATION

One of the world's most spectacular mass
migrations takes place each year in Africa as
an estimated two million animals
travel across the
continent to avoid
the dry season.

Wildebeest, zebras, and gazelles journey more than 1,000 miles (1,600 km) together from the Serengeti in Tanzania to the Maasai Mara in Kenya.

TINY TRAVELER

The ruby-throated hummingbird is a speedy and acrobatic little bird, living in the woodlands and meadows of North America. Its fast-beating wings allow it to hover and dart among trees and flowers.

Every year, the tiny hummingbird sets off on a nonstop 500-mile (800-km) journey across the Gulf of Mexico to spend the winter in a warmer environment.

Before the long flight, it feasts on nectar, insects, and tree sap, almost doubling its bodyweight and building up its strength to help it survive.

These hummingbirds can fly upside down and backward!

A male ruby-throated hummingbird in flight.

BUTTERFLY ROYALTY

Millions of monarch butterflies journey south more than 3,000 miles (4,800 km) each year to avoid the cold winters in the north.

They use air currents to help them to travel up to 100 miles (160 km) in a single day.

These butterfly beauties group together to stay warm, with tens of thousands clinging to a single tree and hanging in colorful clusters.

Many birds group together in flocks for protection, warmth, or to forage for food.

LET'S STICK TOGETHER

When migrating, birds often fly in a special formation to take advantage of air currents.

Tens of thousands of starlings perform stunning displays at dusk, swooping and diving through the air.

A flock of starlings is called a murmuration.

HELPING HANDS

The whooping crane is an endangered species, but scientists have developed a novel way of helping these beautiful birds survive.

It's vital that they migrate for the winter, so ultralight aircraft are used to guide the birds and encourage them to fly south from Wisconsin to Florida.

WATER WORLD

Around 71% of our planet is covered in water, and our oceans, lakes, and rivers are home to some of nature's toughest and most resourceful creatures.

Some are super-speedy swimmers, some undertake marathon migrations halfway around the globe, and others can actually walk on water!

MOONLIGHT JOURNEY

By the light of the moon, female green sea turtles come ashore to dig holes in the sand to lay their eggs before returning to the sea. When the baby turtles hatch, they face a dangerous journey to the water as they try to avoid hungry predators such as seabirds and crabs.

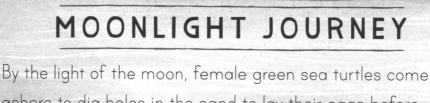

When the time is right, the females will eventually return to the same beach where they hatched in order to lay their own eggs, and a new generation is born.

WATER WADERS

Some reindeer travel up to 3,100 miles (5,000 km) on their annual migration, facing many obstacles, including rivers, lakes, and ocean bays.

Their hollow hairs not only keep them warm, but also help them to float. They use their large hooves to paddle through the water.

The hippopotamus ("river horse" in Ancient Greek) can survive underwater for up to five minutes and is able to close its nostrils and ears to keep the water out.

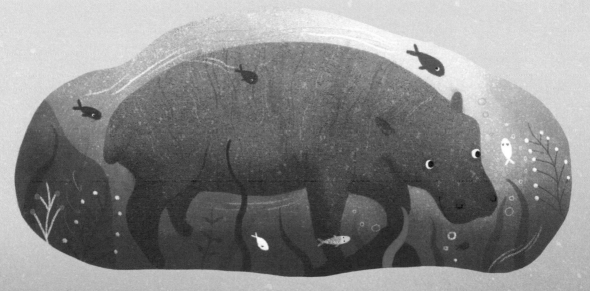

Although they can swim well, hippos often simply walk across the bottom of lakes or rivers in Africa.

SUPER SKATERS

Pond skaters have found their own unique way of traveling — they simply walk on water! They use the surface tension of the water to balance delicately on their long, spindly legs.

The tiny hairs on their legs can sense ripples in the water, alerting the pond skaters to any nearby insects, and their position on the surface means that they are quick to pounce on their prey.

———

This agility also comes in handy when avoiding the attention of predators such as birds, fish, and frogs.

A pond skater catches its prey.

CRABS CROSSING!

Christmas Island in the Indian Ocean is home to tens of millions of red crabs whose annual migration literally stops the traffic!

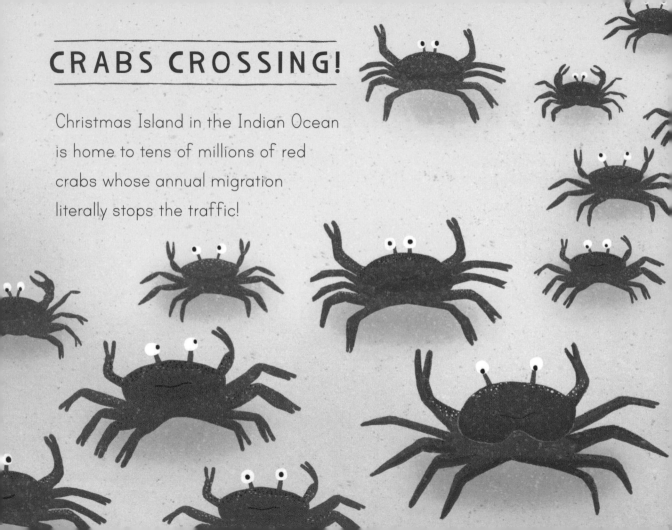

The island's inhabitants have built bridges and underpasses to keep the crabs from being crushed by cars as they make their hazardous journey between the inland forests and the coast to breed.

LARGEST AND LONGEST

Humpback whales can be found in every ocean of the world.

They take part in one of the longest mammal migrations,
traveling an average of 3,100 miles (5,000 km)
to warmer waters near the
equator in order to
breed and give birth
to their young.

CYCLE OF LIFE

The Atlantic salmon swims upriver from the sea to breed and lay her eggs in freshwater.

———

When the eggs hatch, the baby salmon remain in the nest until they become stronger. Once they emerge from the nest, the young fish live for several years in the river until they are big enough to make the long and often perilous journey back to the sea.

———

When they get close to the ocean, the young fish undergo a process called smoltification, allowing their bodies to adapt to the saltwater.

The salmon live in the sea for several years until they are ready to breed. Then they journey upriver to the very same breeding ground where they were born, and the cycle of life begins all over again.

A male Atlantic salmon jumps out of the water.

FUN FACTS

Some seals can dive 3,000 feet (914 m) into the depths of the ocean.

___

The slowest fish is the dwarf seahorse, which travels at only 5 feet (1.5 m) per hour.

___

Male and female walruses migrate separately.

BLOWING HOT AND COLD

The Earth is subject to great extremes in
temperature, from the frozen polar regions
to the intense heat of its deserts.

Some of the most extraordinary animal journeys
take place against the odds in the most
challenging environments.

ADAPTABLE ANIMALS

In extreme conditions, animals must adapt to survive. The camel, which often makes long journeys across the desert, has some special features to help it cope with the conditions.

Its hump is used to store fatty tissue, which can become both a food and water source in dry surroundings. It has nostrils that can close, as well as long, thick eyelashes and a third eyelid to keep out the sand.

The camel's features also make it ideally suited to the icy-cold nighttime temperatures of the desert, as its thick fur keeps it warm.

ON THE HUNT

Most carnivorous animals hunt alone, but some, such as lions, spotted hyenas, and chimpanzees, take part in "cooperative hunting" — working together to trap and capture their prey.

Wolves may roam up to 13 miles (20 km) in a day in their search for food, using their strong sense of smell to stalk their prey. A pack's territory can stretch up to 965 square miles (2,500 sq. km) in the snowy wilderness of Canada and Alaska.

PERSEVERING PENGUINS

Emperor penguins live in the coldest place on Earth, the Antarctic.

Every autumn, they leave the ocean to travel up to 75 miles (120 km) across the sea ice to their breeding grounds.

When their eggs are laid, the female penguins return to the sea, leaving the male penguins to care for the eggs. The male nestles the egg on his feet to protect it and then huddles together with the other male penguins for warmth.

A male penguin protects his chick from the elements.

When the female eventually returns and the chick has hatched, it is the male penguin's turn to trek across the sea ice to the ocean.

————

During the time caring for his chick, the male does not eat, so he may lose up to half his bodyweight. Once back in the sea, he can finally regain his strength by feasting on fish.

DIRTY WORK

Few creatures have a smellier journey than the poor dung beetle, which often lives in hot, dusty environments. "Rollers" do as their name suggests — they roll dung into a ball and use their hind legs to push it along.

They always travel in a straight line — whether or not there's something in their way!

A dung beetle uses his hind legs to roll a ball of dung.

The "tunnellers" bury these dung balls in the ground. They can bury dung weighing 250 times as much as themselves in just one night. And "dwellers" simply live in piles of these delightful dung balls!

———

Some dung beetles use the Sun, the Moon, or even the Milky Way to help navigate their journeys.

———

All this activity makes the dung beetle very useful, because by eating and burying dung, they help to recycle and return nutrients to the soil.

TOO HOT TO HANDLE

In the scorching hot Sahara Desert, the fennec fox has developed thick fur on the soles of its feet in order to protect it as it travels across the hot sand.

———————

Its distinctive large ears have many blood vessels close to the surface, which help keep the fox from overheating by acting as radiators and allowing the heat to escape into the air.

The fennec fox surveys its desert home.

The jerboa, a small rodent resembling a miniature kangaroo, hops around on its long back legs, using its tail for balance. It doesn't need to drink water to survive. Instead, it gets its moisture from food such as plants and insects.

———

The speediest creature on two legs is the ostrich, which can travel at speeds of up to 43 miles per hour (70 kph) — that's pretty fast! Those long legs also come in handy if the ostrich comes under attack, as it uses them to aim hefty kicks at predators.

ON TRACK

Some animal journeys leave very distinctive tracks behind, but it's not always easy to tell what animal was passing through! Can you figure out which creatures made these markings?

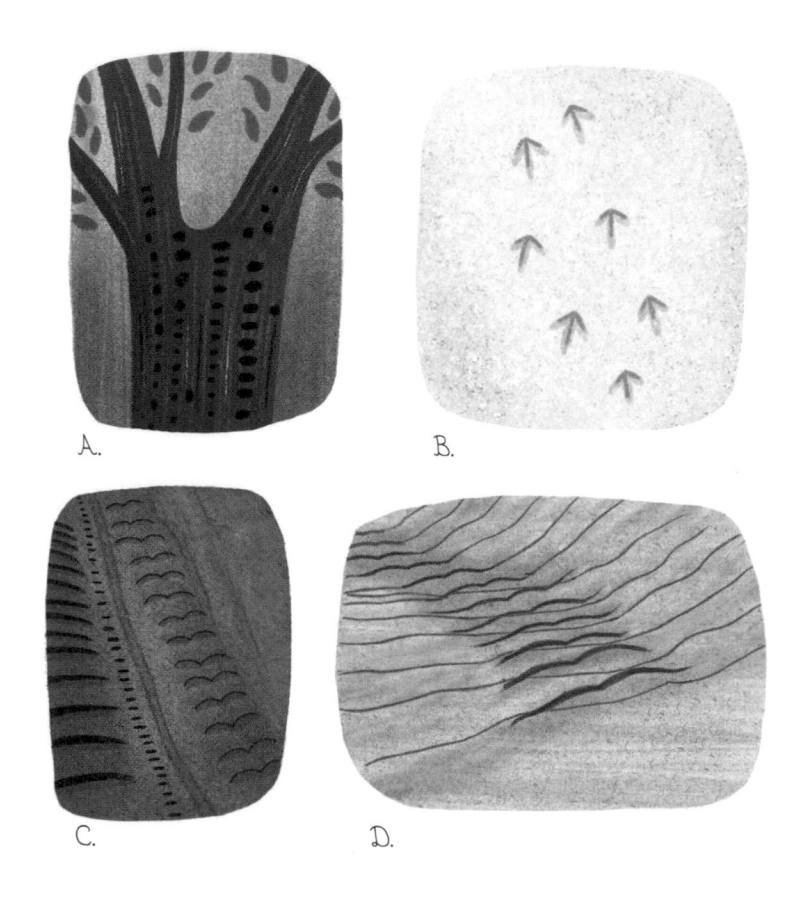

A.

B.

C.

D.

A. woodpecker,   B. bird,   C.   baby green sea turtle,   D. sidewinder snake

44

ANIMAL ANTICS

Some animals may not travel far, but their
journeys are remarkable nonetheless.

———————————

Others have had to adapt to their surroundings in order
to survive, and some are born to be masters of disguise.

———————————

And some animals even seem to have superpowers!
Read on to find out about some rather clever creatures....

FANTASTIC FLYERS

Birds are not the only creatures that like to travel through the air! Flying squirrels have a parachute-like flap of skin stretching from limb to limb, allowing them to glide from tree to tree.

The flying snake from Asia is another glider, flattening its body and forming a concave shape to trap the air. It can even change direction by wriggling around in midair.

The flying fish evades predators by leaping out of the water and using its long wing-like fins to glide above the surface for up to 45 seconds.

Wallace's flying frog, also known as the parachute frog, splays its webbed feet and glides up to 50 feet (15 m) between trees. Special sticky pads on its toes help the frog land safely.

A flying fish.

BUSY BEES

There's a good reason why we talk about being as busy as a bee! The honeybee's journey is vital for the life cycle of plants and flowers.

The female worker bee flies from bloom to bloom, collecting nectar and pollen and pollinating the flowers as she goes.

When she finds a new source of nectar, she returns to the hive and performs a special "waggle" dance to point the other bees in the right direction.

The average bee produces one twelfth of a teaspoon of honey in its lifetime. That's a tiny amount for all that hard work!

SOUND—BOUNCING BATS

Bats are nocturnal, which means that they are active at night.

Bats navigate using a system called echolocation. As they fly, they make a high-pitched cry. This sound bounces off objects and travels back to the bats, helping them to build a mental map of their surroundings and find their way around.

This sonar system also helps them to find and catch prey (mostly insects) as they make their nighttime journeys.

GOING UNDERGROUND

Prairie dogs live in a complex network of tunnels, with separate areas for sleeping, rearing young, and excreting.

Most rabbits live in burrows, which are holes and interconnected passages called warrens. They can be as much as 10 feet (3 m) deep and stretch over large areas.

prairie dog

rabbit

The mole leaves a big clue to the location of its tunnels — a pile of earth known as a molehill can be found at the surface!

The dwarf mongoose often digs its burrows in and around termite mounds. It lives in a family group of up to 40 animals.

It's not just mammals that live underground — burrowing owls like to live in abandoned burrows that have been built by other animals.

mole

dwarf mongoose

burrowing owl

53

I LIKE THE WAY YOU MOVE!

Lamprey eels use undulating, or waving, motions to make the water pull them along.

Scientists believe that caterpillars have a unique "two-body" system of travel, with the caterpillar's gut moving forward separately from the rest of the body and legs.

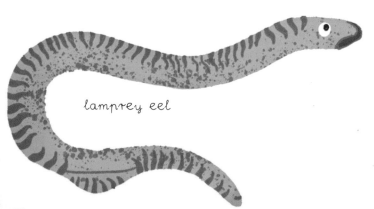

lamprey eel

caterpillar

Earthworms contract and relax their muscles to propel themselves forward in a movement called peristalsis. All this is good for the soil.

Earthworms were called "nature's plows" by Charles Darwin because of the way their movement mixes up different layers of soil and makes it fertile (good for growth).

earthworm

ANT ANTICS

Ants can be found
on every continent
of the world
except Antarctica.

They live in social
groups called colonies.

The largest ant colony
ever discovered was
more than 3,700 miles
(6,000 km) wide.

Ants are surprisingly strong — many can carry 20 times their own bodyweight, and some can carry up to 5,000 times their own bodyweight!

When an ant goes looking for food, it leaves a special scent called a pheromone trail, which leads other ants to the food source.

TRANSFORMATIVE JOURNEY

The butterfly's journey through life is a unique one. It begins with a tiny egg, which eventually hatches into a caterpillar.

The caterpillar munches through leaves until it reaches full size, and then it forms itself into a pupa or chrysalis.

Inside this casing, an amazing transformation takes place. As the case begins to split open, the newly-formed butterfly must wait for its wings to dry before finally taking flight in all its colorful glory.

ARE YOU SITTING COMFORTABLY?

Some animals find that it's easier to catch a ride than travel alone!

Baby kangaroos, known as joeys, ride around in the safety of their mother's pouch until they are brave enough to travel solo. If something alarms them, they will sometimes jump back into the pouch headfirst!

Crabs often hitch a ride on the back of a sea jelly to travel long distances through the water.

A baby koala first travels in its mother's pouch and then ventures onto her back for a piggyback ride as it grows and develops.

ANIMAL MAGIC

Chameleons are born with a range of colors and can change them to match the tones of their surroundings.

Another great master of disguise, the stick insect, blends perfectly into its background of leaves or twigs.

If the best form of defense is attack, the skunk has the right idea, as it sprays a smelly liquid at predators.

The Texas horned lizard goes a step further, spraying blood from its eye sockets!